Hannah-Freya Blake and Edwin Stockdale (eds.)

Sleeping in Frozen Quiet

Indigo Dreams Publishing

First Edition: Sleeping in Frozen Quiet
First published in Great Britain in 2023 by:
Indigo Dreams Publishing
24, Forest Houses
Cookworthy Moor
Halwill
Beaworthy
Devon
EX21 5UU

www.indigodreamspublishing.com

ISBN 978-1-912876-75-4

British Library Cataloguing in Publication Data. A CIP record for this book can be obtained from the British Library.

Designed and typeset in Palatino Linotype by Indigo Dreams.
Cover design by Kathleen Strafford.
Printed and bound in Great Britain by 4edge Ltd.

Papers used by Indigo Dreams are recyclable products made from wood grown in sustainable forests following the guidance of the Forest Stewardship Council.

To the memory of Rev Professor Rosemary Mitchell, dear friend, mentor and colleague, Professor Emeritus of Victorian Studies at Leeds Trinity University and former Director of the Leeds Centre for Victorian Studies (LCVS).

Acknowledgements

The editors would like to extend thanks to the Leeds Centre for Victorian Studies (LCVS) for sponsoring the anthology; to Professor Karen Sayer, Co-Director of the LCVS, for her support; and Rev Professor Jane de Gay, Co-Director of the LCVS, for her support and for writing the introduction. To colleagues in English and Creative Writing at Leeds Trinity University, particularly Professor Oz Hardwick, the series editor of Wordspace, and Dr Amina Alyal for their unflinching enthusiasm and for trusting us with this project. To Kathleen Strafford for her striking cover painting. To Mia Lofthouse for sending the poems on to us anonymously. To IDP for hosting the Wordspace imprint. To the Brontës for their brilliant imagination. To all the contributors for allowing us to engage with your creative work.

CONTENTS

Sleeping in Frozen Quiet

-

Foreword

To many people with a passing knowledge of the Brontë Sisters, their story is overshadowed by death – or, to be precise, multiple deaths. Their home at the Parsonage in Haworth, where their father Revd Patrick Brontë was perpetual curate, adjoined a graveyard that was 'terribly full of upright tombstones', as Elizabeth Gaskell put it.[1] It sets the scene for a grim roll-call: elder sisters Maria (1814-1825) and Elizabeth (1815-1825) died while they were schoolgirls; the only brother Branwell (1817-1848) died of tuberculosis and addiction fuelled by disappointment in love; Emily (1818–1848) succumbed to tuberculosis induced, the story goes, by standing in the cold at her brother's funeral. Anne (1820–1849) retreated to Scarborough for her health but found the journey so traumatic that she died not long after arriving there. Charlotte (1816–1855), the only sibling to be married, died along with unborn child during pregnancy.

Despite this, it would be hard to find nineteenth-century writers who are more alive than the Brontës. Like Cathy and Heathcliff who do not sleep in the 'quiet earth' but perpetually roam the moors together at the end of *Wuthering Heights,* and in the spirit of Jane Eyre's epitaph to her friend Helen Burns, *'Resurgam'* (I will rise again), the Brontës and their works have frequently been brought to life in film and theatre, and they have inspired numerous creative pieces including, for example, *Wide Sargasso Sea* by Jean Rhys (1966), *The Lost Child* by Caryl Phillips (2015), and *Reader, I Married Him* (2016), a collection of stories edited by Tracy Chevalier as a companion piece to her exhibition for Charlotte's bicentenary at the Brontë Parsonage Museum.

This collection of poems continues the tradition of celebrating the continuing presence of the Brontës. Maura

---

[1] *The Life of Charlotte Brontë* (1857; Harmondsworth: Penguin, 1985), p. 56.

Dooley sets the tone with a popular epitaph from World War I, copied by her grandmother into what must have been a centenary edition of the Brontë novels: 'Nearer than the living are the unforgotten dead. / Their presence is ever with you / and they walk always at your side.' Mark Connors imagines Emily telling Heathcliff that she created him so that she could be 'immortal like you.' And Lucy Wright captures the afterlife of the Brontës in her wonderful oxymoron, 'To breathe between the pages now a posthumous ode.'

Furthermore, there is a vigour in many of the Brontë works that tempts readers to let down their post-structuralist guard in order to cheerfully confuse authors and characters and to see both characters and authors as 'real' people. Many people feel as Virginia Woolf did when reading *Jane Eyre* that the 'writer has us by the hand, forces us along her road, makes us see what she sees, never leaves us for a moment or allows us to forget her.'[2] Holly Bars speaks for many when she articulates her own relationship with Charlotte Brontë and Jane Eyre across the generations: 'I hold her close to me; I feel her beating in my chest.' Nowhere are the Brontës more present than at Haworth, and several poems in this collection are pieces of psychogeography that seek out intimations and sightings on Haworth Moor, Top Withens (the subject of two poems), and the Parsonage (two poems, one of which takes us to the heart of the home, on Emily's beloved sofa). Wendy Pratt imagines the Brontës being free to roam the Parsonage again when lockdown kept the tourists away. Other poems capture the texture of the north of England, its landscape and its language; Helen Hill presents Heathcliff as a product of the land, 'carved … out / from Haworth moor, hard as grit, / stubborn as stone.' Edwin Stockdale combines psychogeography with ekphrasis with his creative response to both Haworth Moor and Anne Brontë's *The Tenant of Wildfell Hall* in 'The Last Fall of Snow'.

---

[2] *'Jane Eyre* and *Wuthering Heights'*, *Collected Essays* (London: Hogarth, 1966), 4 vols., Vol. 2, p.186.

Of course, the Brontës sing the most powerfully through their own words and Stockdale's poem, like many others in this collection, is a feast of intertextuality. From the book's title (a phrase from *The Tenant of Wildfell Hall*) onwards, poets snip and curate lines from the Brontës' work to creative effect. Some of these are clearly identified in titles or footnotes: Claire Wigzell's 'The Soaring Rooks' has many qualities of a found poem; Hannah Stone's 'From Verdopolis to *Villette*' allows the imaginary worlds and words of Charlotte's juvenilia to mingle with her mature novel *Villette,* but also with her everyday life, as indeed the Brontës allowed their imaginations to add colour to their quotidian existence. Oz Hardwick brings *Villette* into dialogue with *I Ching* under the influence of Syd Barrett. Many of the poems have a rich loam of buried allusions, where the words of the Brontës are allowed to echo through, inviting readers to do their own detective work, make their own connections, and draw their own conclusions.

The collection was conceived at the moment when the series of bicentenary celebrations was drawing to a close: the last one, for Anne – in the spirit of perpetuity – took place in 2021 rather than 2020, due to the pandemic. Many of the poems therefore reimagine the Brontës and their work from the perspective of twenty-first-century concerns and critical enquiries. The Caribbean origins of *Jane Eyre's* 'madwoman in the attic' Bertha Mason accrue new poignancy in the wake of Black Lives Matter: Jenny Mitchell alerts the reader to the possibility that Bertha's brother 'Mason hangs more slaves than anyone / around, bodies left to rot / out on the lawn.' Concerns to explore masculinities are now integral to gender debates that had once been decidedly feminist: Rochester, Arthur Huntingdon, and Heathcliff all appear here in a new light of uncertain identity and fragile masculinity. Branwell emerges with more nuance and subtlety than the judgemental picture painted by Gaskell; indeed his struggle for selfhood and identity was more urgent than that of his sisters, as Amina Alyal reminds us. Like the cover illustration of this book, the poems put Branwell back into the famous 'pillar portrait' of his sisters, from which he had blotted out his own image. *The Tenant of Wildfell Hall* is queered by Gregory Wood, who suggests that bringing up a boy as a 'Miss Nancy' may be no bad thing.

The contributors to this collection draw their inspiration from a wide range of Brontë creations, and this, too, reflects recent shifts in critical attention that give weight to the full range of their output. Contributors frequently allude to the Juvenilia, set in the lands of Gondal, created by Anne and Emily, and Angria, created by Charlotte and Branwell, the latter of whom wrote himself into the story through the character and *nom de plume* Northangerland. (Su Ryder captures the tantalizing, fragmentary nature of these early writings in 'Elegy'.) The best-known novels, Emily's *Wuthering Heights* and Charlotte's *Jane Eyre,* are present it is true, but lesser-known novels have new prominence: Charlotte's *Shirley* (set at the time of the Luddite Riots), with its argumentative curates and its heroines Caroline Helstone and Shirley Keeldar, and *Villette,* with its unlikely hero Monsieur Paul and its uncertain ending which subverts the tidy 'Reader I married him' conclusion of *Jane Eyre.* (Peter Donnelly blends literary criticism, metafiction and poetry to explore this in 'My Readers'.) Anne Brontë was for many generations such a shadowy figure that one of the early studies was titled *The Other One* (Elizabeth Langland, 1989), but critics are now taking her seriously, and the collection acknowledges this with allusions to *Agnes Grey* but more pertinently with references to her courageous championing of a woman's right to leave an abusive marriage in *Tenant of Wildfell Hall.*

This book is a sequel to *An Insubstantial Universe* (2020), a poetry anthology in celebration of George Eliot on the bicentenary of her birth, edited by Edwin Stockdale and Amina Alyal. Like the earlier volume, this is a collaboration between two centres of excellence at Leeds Trinity University: the Leeds Centre for Victorian Studies (LCVS) and the Creative Writing

Group that hosts Wordspace (two monthly open mic evenings, one online and one in the local community), as well as BA and MA programmes and PhD opportunities. The contributors to this volume include poets who perform regularly at Wordspace, as well as pieces solicited by the editors, and poems selected from responses to a public call for papers. The Leeds Centre for Victorian Studies is an internationally-recognized centre of excellence in the discipline, running conferences, seminars and colloquia, as well as offering Masters by Research and PhD opportunities. Like *An Insubstantial Universe,* this collection reflects the mission of the LCVS to question and traverse disciplinary boundaries. It also cuts across boundaries of literary and historical periods to find that the Brontës are indeed alive and thriving in the twenty-first century.

Revd Professor Jane de Gay, October 2022

The Unforgotten – Maura Dooley

At Anne Brontë's grave, in the salt air she loved,
where the words were almost lost from the stone,
dissolving, you first kissed me
           and once, we took my parents to see
the rain, the moorland, the tiny writing we struggled to read,
stepping out dazed into that garden of tombs
gleaming, in the damp light
           and sometimes, I swipe at crumbs or dry plates
with my souvenir linen image of three melded heads,
fading, indistinct,
           but today, I open a beaten copy
of *The Novels of the Brontë Sisters* (Pilot 1947),
the only thing left of my Grandmother's time on earth,
to read, in her bold emphatic hand,
'Nearer than the living are the unforgotten dead.
Their presence is ever with you
and they walk always at your side.'

Elegy – Su Ryder

Hive imagination,
contained, restrained, and curbed by small-world cobbles,
swells, inflames, erodes judgemental dams,
cemetery walls, parochial patter.

Ravens, rooks or razorbills, the cries
echo the same frustrations. Aspiration,
clogged by convention, repression, tradition,
will fail. Succumb to simple human suffering.

Only shrugging off this mundane skin,
achieves release. Deflated, spent and hacking,
masking, battling, reeling uphill, ranting.
Ruins of unfinished fantasies.

Now Angria and Gondal lie encrypted
in bones. The shrieking, creaking, carrion eaters
mourn. Fuss through life's leavings. History,
pecked apart by pilgrims and sea frets.

My Readers – Peter Donnelly

Did he drown at sea,
or come back and marry her?
is what they always ask,
never wonder why I said
he *was* away three years,
not *has been*, but *he is coming.*
They assume, I think,
at least when they read it the second time,
that I'm still in Villette at the end,
though I'm writing in English.
Do they forget my saying
since those days I have seen the West End,
or do they think that's an oversight
on the part of my creator?
I never actually confirmed
that Madame Beck had died,
nor Pere Silas, just that they
prospered all the days of their lives,
though I made it clear several chapters back
that my godmother and Mr Home
were no longer with us,
that Graham and Paulina's children
had grown up. They could be grandparents,
as could I – I said my hair
was grey, or white.
It puzzles me why so many
think it's set in France,
though the priest was French,
a foreigner just like me;
had he been a native,
I couldn't have confided in him,
another thing they forget I told them.
A lot to take in, I know,

and much of it confusing,
but you might find your essay easier
if you remember the bits that are not.

Chapter 38: Divergence – Oz Hardwick

The drug wrought in the green chorus, a strange basin of strengthening at the altar. Roots owned illumination, and some level of estrangement showed in the breaking of the summer park, with its long dreams all silent, lone and safe. That Heaven I knew, and I had often stood, part of the natural order, a deep stranger in the blazing sea, fire ascending and water descending. Brimming with cool, I knew my midnight, framing the tremulous song of teeming rubies. Countless sisters crowded the wild lake and the rushy vision was a concert, with all its tidings building architectural harmonies from torches and trumpets in swaying shadows, sparking horses whose riders swept back like golden sparks. I followed voices until it seemed the shade, the sweet tide, rose in shadows, rushing swiftly on scores of symbols that must have been dropped like grand masks in the open glare. The sphynx had once told me at the altar that there are always creative possibilities inherent in polarities, and what I heard was, I think, the wild plain sound of the land, space, a Byzantine obelisk, and glass palaces of gemming moonlight. The whole sound was abroad: meteors and gay trees. Simply put, when people grow apart – even for the most natural of reasons – their points of view, values, interests and schedules diverge. In this midnight, mid-century vision of the storm, the enchanted were shadowy and calm. There, at least, were neither fires nor alleys.

Cf. Charlotte Brontë, Villette *(1853) and the* I Ching *or* Book of Changes *(circa 1000-750 BCE). With thanks to Roger Keith "Syd" Barrett (1946-2006).*

The Heat and Violence of a Poet's Heart – Amina Alyal
(Virginia Woolf, quoted by Apignanesi in Gilbert and Gubar)

> 'the "bad animal" who was first locked up in the red-
> room is, we sense, still lurking somewhere…'
> Gilbert and Gubar, *The Madwoman in the Attic.*

Second-wave ears tune themselves in to uncanny laughter
scuttling behind the wainscot in reception rooms, mirth
flaring up into flames, laughs praeternatural in bondage.

Unlikely, in the North's wild wuthering and ice-dimmed air,
that such ire-stoked furnaces should flourish, such anger slip
like salamanders loosed in the grouse in a gorse-filled fell.

Waterloo, Peterloo, *the same peal, the same low, slow ha! ha!*
What sparks Angria, Gondal, Glass Town, Northangerland,
the heavy tolling of names, *Heathcliff, Mason, the West Indies -* ?

There's the freight of plantations, the weight of St Peter's Fields,
the borne guilt of the gilded few, weighing them down, all
searing the towering Houses, bringing down rooftop in rubble.

Ah, then, *millions are in silent revolt against their lot*; their plight
oppresses the child, burns in her eyes as she contemplates pens,
but it is Branwell who cries *O ANGRIA ARISE!* whose alias,

Northangerland, versifies rather than totting up columns,
writes books when he needs to be keeping them, takes tots
of laudanum, pheromones, hellfire, every kind of drink, lost.

Charlotte Uncaged – Maggie Mackay

I am no bird; and no net ensnares me.

Paper lovers, burning letters, suffering,
she writes wild torch songs, of mad desire.

Bertha, Jane, Rochester, silently pierced
with passion, ooze earthly sunlit lust.

Her hot words soar above charismatic pages
in bold patterns, textured floods of love.

Her power is the fire of pen and black ink,
intimacy, leather bound in fixed print.

Bad Boys – Deborah A Lyons

'For there is no limit to the wild extravagance of hope's imaginings,'
says Arthur Huntingdon in Anne Brontë's *The Tenant of Wildfell Hall*.

There's something about a bad boy.
Clever women have always known this.
The kind riding high in the saddle,
looking down with brooding arrogance
and the certainty of his quarry.
Or the one caught in a maelstrom of appetite,
flung around by gigantic loves,
untamed and scornful of expectations.
How gorgeous is the Byronesque,
slapping slick leather gloves,
all robust strength and impulsive passions.

Small wonder those shackled
by stifling faith and propriety
jumped aboard the coattails of these men.

But in our times will these men
still exude an enduring allure?
TV screens flicker with eye-lined
images of Johnny Depp
but the wives will leave.
Clever women come to know this.

A Controversy – Gregory Woods

(The Tenant of Wildfell Hall)

You say his mother mollycoddles him
and spoils the raw material for what
was meant to be a man. Indulgent but
resolved, she guides his path: she never lets
him struggle on his own. He runs the risk,
so used to her maternal sycophancy,
of being thought—and she of being blamed
for having made of him—a mere *Miss Nancy*.

But what of that? Worse things have come of love,
and there are tougher fates than being called
a milksop! So, although a man should lurk
discreetly on the plainer side of fancy,
a lot of us would be perversely proud
to live up to the honour of *Miss Nancy*.

Pillar – Carole Bromley

Branwell was the one that interested me,
the prodigal, the indulged and only son,
the one who returned home carrying shame

into that ordered tick-tock vicarage
where the rooms were always too small for him.
One look at that panelled coffin-bed

and I don't buy his father's glum withdrawal,
his sisters' loyal, purse-lipped tolerance.
Instead, I hear angry voices echo

from those polished copper porridge pans.
Be a man! All that money down the drain.
Branwell, in his room, scrubbing himself out.

The Masons of Spanish Town – Jenny Mitchell

It's widely said they are not white,
not deeply in the bones. Black blood
runs through the Mason veins on both sides,
despite their fields stretched out for miles,
a wealth of white-gold cane.

The house is rich and grand, each room
made dark with oils, great portraits
frowning at the English oak that creaks
with loyalty – *God Save the King!*
Mice refuse all meals except high tea.

Mason hangs more slaves than anyone
around, bodies left to rot
out on the lawn. As a sign of strength,
peacocks peck the dangling feet,
drunk with the taste of blood.

But the hint of black repels the white
elite, proud of their tissue-paper skin,
curling in the sun, they order maids to sneer
when Masons come to call,
doors slammed on reddened faces.

Maids spread these rumours too –
Masons in the past where slaves,
concubines who whored for land.
Dangerous the way they fade,
descended over time.

Northangerland – Bob Beagrie

Reddish brown, extremely bitter, remote enough
to dampen screams, the island tremors
in a pan of steam – a canker in a crook of moor,

all juniper berries and poppy vales
dissolving within stoppered vial

such mischief comes, self-inflicted, daily harms
to soothe the hurt, just one more sip to numb
the nerves. I'll become King between four walls.
The Bedraggled Duke of Bedclothes, sick sick

sick of the how they shake their heads, purse
their lips in disdain; sweet sisters, who've learned
to act a better man, with restraint, better
at recalling the rhyme and treason of decorum,

for there's no respectability in cholera,
there being no decency in consumption,

especially now I'm wasted by delirium,
shed from Lydia's living prison, stripping coyly,
lit by candlelight, hair loosened on my breast,
lathered from warming skin with sin,

covert love, pick-pocketed from behind rainfall,
snowdrift, night-gale whisperings when circumstance
turns the master's balding head, the furtive chase,

the strike like rabbit scamperings as a white owl
wheels across the heath, hunger in every
lingering touch as we pledged one other empires

though the world but lasts one swallow, one spit,
leaving behind it such cravings for this bitter tincture,
reddish brown, remote enough to dampen screams.

From Verdopolis to Villette – Hannah Stone

Zenobia glided past proud salons, glittering with chandeliers whose bright beams gleamed on the jewel-coloured cushions heaped on silken ottomans; the warmth from the brilliant fires ignited a pearly glow on her soft cheeks. Her golden curls caress'd a snow-white brow, whose animation arose from a pair of deepest blue eyes.

She puts down her pen. Chilblains throb on her toes; her father had burned the bright boots given to protect the tiny feet of the vicarage children from wet moors. He had shredded his wife's silk gown. Had he been able to reach above the wild empty currents of Yorkshire air, he would have switched off the sun, rather than have it indulge his children, make them soft. But he lets them have pens; in their little hands, they are keys, and she becomes more than merely small and plain.

Brussels, March 6th, 1843
The Carnival is just over and we have entered upon the gloom and abstinence of Lent. For breakfast today there was coffee, without milk; vinegar and vegetables, with a very little salt fish for dinner; and bread for supper.

The porridge was sent up not merely burned, but thickened with offensive fragments of unknown origin; how their empty stomachs clenched shut at the very smell of it. Back home, the yeasty odour fills the room from its damp flags to its cramped ceiling. Emily, who is pummelling the dough, looks beyond the bowl, to the book propped against the flour bin. The bread rises.

Zamorna lifts the delicate vessel of succulent chocolate; within reach of his scented fingers, a dozen golden plover eggs nestle in their folded damask shroud, awaiting their opportunity to tempt his palate.

She retches, continuously. Dares no longer hope that the small tenant of her long vacant womb will thrive. Her gullet rises, again; her pulse flutters to a cadence. Above the stone coffin of all her keenly-fought victories, the surprising joy, the truncated hopes, a lark spins its breathless song.

Note: passages in italics are quotations (verbatim or close) from Charlotte Brontë's juvenilia, and her letters, as recorded by Elizabeth Gaskell in her *Life of Charlotte Brontë*.

Anne by Candlelight – Lucy Wright

Fiction of the written word, bound by paperback, explores worlds that are not too unfamiliar of our own. In the imaginary homages of hometowns, Haworth, and halls. Existing in the liminal spaces of lines that hold real testaments to the wants and needs of women wrapped in prose at Wildfell Hall, within the English gentry, and Victorian literature. Prose that is sharply written in premature irony of Romanticism. Revolutionary writing amongst a name as familiar as the Classics that line our shelves.

Anne is writing inside of writing, as a woman is inside herself. She is intertextual. Part-epistolary, private, personal. Full of splendour. Revealing and relishing as a woman should have been, by candlelight with pen and ink.
> *"Simple and beautiful as a muslin dress."*

Talent amongst the tumultuous tales of life. Amongst tuberculosis. In the chaos of drafts and tear-stained pages she made for a manuscript to spot herself in. A masterpiece, a revelation, perfectly crafted in the dampness of an empty office. A desk by a bedroom window with fingers too cold to hold a pen in winter. Bringing colour to unadulterated canvases. A voice on paper for the often-forgotten sister. A Brontë whose first name is found between paragraphs of the most beautiful prose. It is not us as the eye of the beholder, the critic that sees the errors in her misunderstood shapes. It is Anne, who burns brightly by that candlelight. Who does not weigh her merits against her sisters, amongst the battle of the Brontë girls. Her name prevails from a parish in West Yorkshire, to the tongues of women and devotees a bicentenary later. As an individual with a voice that will be captured in semi colon sentences.

To not relinquish the writing. To cherish. To breathe between the pages now a posthumous ode. Authored by a pen wrapped in silk. Bleeding onto calico.

Heathcliff – Helen Hill

Whose hand was this that chiselled you
from wind and weather, carved you out
from Haworth moor, hard as grit,
stubborn as stone?

Who made you, child of Satan,
brute and brutalised,
charismatic lover and abuser,
to haunt us still?

Emily forged you, her frail hand
wringing you from the landscape
as storms raged within, without,
the parsonage walls

as she longed for it all
to end, her own dear ghosts
to beckon at the window pane,
for snow to fall, deep snow.

Burning – Hannah-Freya Blake

Mad, bad, and dangerous to know:
the men swagger in their stride
with Byronic brooding brow and burning eyes –
blink once for yes, ladies, and twice as well,
since silence has as much to tell
where "no" left echoes in the walls
and fingernails turned to cat-like claws.

Mad, bad, and dangerous to know:
the women with passion in their eyes,
confined to bedlam beds and closeted attic wives –
burn the curtains, Bertha, and then the lot,
since Rochester abandoned you to rot,
while Cathy could cry murder on the moors
and *tap, tap, tap* on Heathcliff's windows and doors.

Slags, hags and blaspheming bitches:
the women who were burnt and hung as witches
with too much to say, with too few fucks given
for that "masucline" temperament of creative ambition –

curse, conjure and bewitch!
poison with every laughing kiss!

But most of all, in my humble opinion,
consider pen and paper your greatest minions
as nothing is braver for women who think
than to write their truth in Bible-black ink.

The Last Fall of Snow – Edwin Stockdale

iron sky of winter // blighted fields // horizon and hills one bitter whirl of suffocating snow // a hoary mass gleams through the darkness // a crowd of snow-clad trees // remote call of the swollen beck // I listen like the evening and winter-wolf snuffling the snow scenting prey // starlight and the cold reflection from snow in our chamber // the glass of flowers the carmine snow and gold of petals // a tall sable-robed snow-veiled woman steals through the casement

Note: the title is a quotation from Chapter 7 of Anne Brontë's *The Tenant of Wildfell Hall*. The other phrases are taken from all 7 of the Brontë sisters' novels.

Charlotte, Readying – Donna Irving

I shall leave on a neap tide,
be separated by waves,
carry dialect under my tongue.
I sew moorland air into hems and collars,
rub curlew song into my core.
A talisman of peat hangs around my neck.
I stitch each vista behind my eyes,
store millstone grit beneath my nails.
Under the arch of each foot,
I carve my deep valley.
Each shoe I tie with train whistles.
I pull on my jacket of rain.
And you, you I ink upon my soul.

Haworth Moor – Alison Milner

The wind flings words here –
they braid stalks of grass
flutter papery leaves
glide the fustian moor.

The beck sings words here –
they are bit by ice
spat by torrential rain
shredded dry in sun.

The stone seeps words here –
they are hewn from rock
carved by millstone grit –
particles of the dead.

The words settle here –
they are crows perching
curlews circling sky
moss spores weaving prose.

North – Penny Boxall
(after 'The North Wind' by Anne Brontë)

Now that it is out of hand, entirely wild,
it is not enough to think that the wind
blasting me on this northerly fellside
(streaming the brown flag of my hair,
mocking my 'windproof' jacket)
has already glossed over things I love.
I want them here —
                        the tarn with only
a moorhen dipping between lilypads;
a November morning in which
the puddles and roots freeze, shine;
a particular blackbird whose canny face
was always there…
                      The wind is trying.
Like a cat it carries voices
from the next ridge over,
lays them at my feet in tenderness.
Or it could be warning.

She was a Wild Wicked Slip – Kathleen Strafford

In me there is something dangerous
a cruelty growing
you taught me how to be ruthless
        look how our heather withers

If I were a painter
        I'd paint you
            on the moors
            under stormy skies
            stabbing
            your own beating heart
            & pleased with your deed
            squeeze mine to bursting
forcing the tempest of clouds to stand still
as love's blood spurts
        across our grief-stricken canvas

The devil take thy soul!
                do not leave me in the abyss
                    rise out of your grave
                        or let me be buried quick with you!

If I could touch myself the way you touch me
I wouldn't need you to return
                but I do
You're the one I'm drawn to
I'll wring kisses from your lips & throat
Your ghost speaks in panes & mirrors
                pricks like nettles
                my hands are wet with tears
                        as you tap   tap   tap

Top Withens – Will Kemp

We came here once, years ago;
played tig about the stones, imitated
ghosts through paneless windows.

And now I'm back on the moor,
the evening sky clear but for the spray
of a cloud far above, barely there –

my mind darkening with the years
of not knowing if she lived, but longing
to glimpse her face once more –

the bright sun long since gone
and a north wind picking up behind
as I begin to head back down the valley.

The Soaring Rooks – Clare Wigzell

Not rich enough to own a watch, she only
knew the time from the slow lengthening
shadows she could see from the window.

The high wall with a massive wooden gate,
cast a darkness that took possession
of the whole ground, forcing the golden sunlight
to retreat, inch by inch, and take refuge at last
in the very tops of the trees. A colony of noisy
rooks were reduced, a few moments later,
to the sombre worky-day hue of the lower world,
her own world within. Dreary it was to dwell
on the dull, grey, desolate path before her.

As she watched, a few birds soared above,
receiving again, the lustre of the sun, which imparted
to their sable plumage the brilliance of deep red gold.
She felt the purity and freshness of air, breeze
enough to ripple feathers, precious moments
of warmth, the wide view beyond the park,
of fields and moor.

This scene, like a flint and steel,
fell on the tinder of her wishes, igniting the flame
of hope within.

Note: This poem is made up, mostly, with words from *Agnes Grey* by Anne Brontë.

Rhythms – Jill Lang

(after 'Home' by Anne Brontë)

The woodland ivy plays still
along dry-stone walls,
rain slipping from tearful trees.

Anne watches from the window,
glimpses bob of father's hat. Waits, hears
solemn step in hallway, shut of study door.

She regains fireside rocker,
returns to Gondal, distance broken
by quiet cough louder than words.

'Farewell to thee but not farewell' – Eva Wigzell

Air is thin as I breathe
in and out like weary waves far below.
And I fear it is now I must go.

Clutching my shawl around me,
I am still.

Watching from my window
the German Sea beneath.
Dark waters whipped up by coarse winds.
Heavy clouds trouble the clear vast blue
with deep grey.

Cliffs are smacked with foaming sea
thrusting its rage on the jagged, unfeeling face.
The waves have more to say.
A spit and slosh of protest.

The sand beneath slipping, left bare.

But though I must fall away
my spirit is steadfast like the cliff
and the sand is never left dry for long.
I am still.

Take courage, Charlotte, take courage.

My Mother Re-launches Herself – Sheila Jacob

She catches a train at New Street,
changes at Harrogate for Haworth,
checks in at her Bed & Breakfast.

She's Sheila's mother. Pat's widow.
Margaret, the quietly-spoken woman
recently retired from Lewis's department store
where she worked in the staff canteen,
portioned fish, chips and mushy peas
onto the plates of ladies from lingerie.

Next morning, she combs her hair,
washes her face, adds a dusting of Crème Puff.
No lipstick, no perfume, no jewels
except a gilt cross around her neck.

It's the Brontë Society's AGM
and her first time this far north.
She left school at fourteen,
speaks unashamed Brummie,
but feels undaunted by the thought
of academics flocking together,
chirping in cut-glass accents.

She's read all the books,
keeps a copy of Emily's poems
on her bedside table,
prefers *Villette* to *Agnes Grey*
and Mr. Rochester to Professor Emanuel.

She buttons up her coat, takes her handbag,
steps from the horse and trap
and stands outside the candlelit window
of Thornfield Hall.

The Brontës in Lockdown – Wendy Pratt

The sisters seep from the walls
like the scent of old clothes,
slight as candle whisps at first,
then thickening in the air
around the table.

They crowd the window, skirt
against skirt; are surprised
by the trees in the churchyard,
by the number of headstones
by the neat frame of the garden.

Charlotte runs a finger down the books,
along the oval of her portrait. Emily reaches
for a dog that isn't there.
Upstairs, Branwell opens cupboards
and drawers. Some insatiable need
drives him like a poltergeist. Anne shifts
in her seat, cocks her head
to the sound of a lone seagull.

The velvet rope is solid as ever
holding them in place. They remain
behind it, tethered like horses
waiting for their owners to return.

The Living Room Sofa, Haworth Parsonage – Helen Kay

The green sofa's mahogany arms
curl, firmly maternal as snail shells.
Prompted by signs, we picture its story.

I.
Inky pages on the table, the sisters sink
into the sofa's lap, to conjure Mrs Reed
on her ottoman, Cathy soaked on a settle.

II.
It bears Emily's pale wheezing frame.
Nursing her in this room of new chapters
lets them all forget how she slips away.

III.
A threadbare father has mourned
too much; this couch is a dusky witness
bearing its own heavy emptiness.

IV.
The arms fossilise to gravestones
by a velvet heath that calls ghost names,
let us make them flesh. Can you hear?

Roaming – Jenny Robb

I hear the sea,
not false waves of wind
through trees.

I respond
to elemental force
sculpting across centuries,

not tied to earth by family
where my heart, now dust,
might mingle with brother
and sisters.

I am ironstone,
embedded in limestone.
I am separated from you all
by more than my Scarborough grave.

Top Withens – Clint Wastling

The hailstones of July
sting bare flesh prepared
for summer in the village.
Wind stirs up from the moor
driving sunlight before it
as clouds coalesce beyond the ridge.

We are equipped with boots,
cagoules, a thermos
but the rain saturates,
drives rivulets along
lines of weakness.
We take shelter in the ruins.

The young man shivers
no match for the wild weather.
I offer a warm drink,
which he accepts with a bow.
He is a Japanese student
studying the sisters, he's reading Anne.

The storm will pass
like Huntingdon's rages,
the sun returns to brighten the bracken.
We follow storm clouds downhill,
a coach waits with steamed up windows
bored faces looking on.

Tellint Tale – Sarah Wimbush

On allut childers, tis Emily
owd Tabby sees – made kin o me –
swore starve if Ars be set adrift,
kept hars wi me und scrubbed n pressed.

Pillin tatties agint range
Ar sees Miss loike a she-bear caged,
n yet still yon bitti mouse: mystry
shoo wor ter arn kith but nart wi me,

Ar knewd shoo loved em tales be told
o - beggin God's pardon – boggarts,
heath fairies, sowls narght this earth,
human nature undreamt, cussed,

n all ot flaysome gooins on
from Haworth top to Keighley tarn.
N whet Ar hears em breath ont page
me thinks o Miss gallopin aways

arght ont heath; wind agatherin
up wit curlews n them thear wailins,
hor skirts gone agin Top Withens
tilt moore n Missie Em but one.

Look Who's Back – Mark Connors

After rave reviews on Trip Advisor,
he opts for *Cobbles and Clay.*
The falafel wrap is to die for,
Washed down with a Chai Soya Latte.
He was dairy-free before his time;
he never knew a mother's milk.
After finishing his dark Belgian torte,
he sneers the room. All they do his clap.
They think it's all part of a Haworth day trip,
like he's some RADA trained thespian,
low on his luck. He starts to rant at them.
They lap it up like salted caramel foam.
They have no idea his heart is as black
as his cloak. He rises to a standing ovation

then rages out on to the cobbled street,
barges through a convoy of ramblers,
storms up to the pub to drown his wrath.
The place is packed with families,
nippers eating beige food not fit for farm hands,
let alone Hareton Earnshaw. *Damn you all*, he screams,
before snatching a pint from the hands of a bloke.
He necks it, smithereens the glass into the hearth.

At The Parsonage, he sees Nelly Dean,
talking shite, as usual, while mixing cake batter.
He stops her mid-tale and her audience gasps.
'Where's my Cathy?' he howls.
'You might catch her at the weekend, love.
The woman who plays her won't be here till Sunday.
Emily's in the other room, if that's any good.'
And there she is, his creator, sitting at a table,
writing in one of her tiny books.

'Why did you make me?' he growls.

'Why?' she says. 'To be immortal like you.'

Writing Broken-hearted – Angela Topping

Not just the wide moors and hard-bitten country
but Yorkshire mills, factory floors,
machinery and the fight for rights.

Not just romance but humour of curates
covering the town like snow on hills
waiting for Charlotte to write them.

Her own Mr Nicholls not so quarrelsome.
He relished her sharp portrayals,
knowing she didn't mean *him.*

While she wrote, her world fell apart:
Branwell, Emily, Anne all hacking blood,
succumbing to the illness they dreaded.

All she could do, to escape the grief, was write.
In the numb blankness of the house's silence,
the only sounds were her pen scritch-scratching,

relentless clock marking time, father
alone with his books, softly breathing,
the fire, and wind soughing round the house.

Did her tears blot the pages, as she thought of
her sisters writing beside her no more,
their comradely appreciation of each other?

Or did she choke her tears in the writing
as Caroline and Shirley talk of poetry.
Cowper's hand did not tremble in writing the lines.

Women for whom the Bells Toll – Rachel Davies

Currer wrote Jane, plain of face,
poor of purse, but feisty, intelligent,
a feminist icon who lives by her wits;
a smouldering babe in a governess gown
swept along like a pedalo on an ocean of passion
for her bigamist lover, his shame in the attic.
In the end, reader, she marries him.

Ellis wrote Cathy, reckless and schizoid,
aspiring to gentility but riven by obsession
for a dark, moody Other, lost piece in her jigsaw.
Her longing will kill her. She'll call to her man
not from Heaven or Hell but the unconstrained
afterlife of a Wuthering moor where she'll roam
with her soul mate, the dangerous Heathcliff.

Acton wrote Agnes, sweet and submissive.
For three hundred pages she preaches to the reader
about being a Good Girl, the sure path to heaven,
administers her sermon, weak tea with four sugars,
as a remedy for the shock induced by her sisters.
Reader, don't drink her; when nobody's looking
tip her into the aspidistra, suck up the strong women.

The Tenant – Gill Lambert

Drink and infidelity pass down
from father to his son, she's seen it
in her own kind; attracts the same kind.

She marks herself safe from every
weekend piss-up, glad he's too far gone
to lift his fists. Still, she knows this time
might be the one, watched by his son,

learning the trade of being a man
by his father's hands; how cheap,
how easy women are. How little

it takes. And every grotty hovel
damp-walled rental flips him closer
to an edge she's scared of falling from.

So she leaves him, takes her boy
and her belongings, changes her name
to hide her past and save her reputation.

Men pull in all directions, love
and truth are close accomplices,
retribution isn't always fairly dealt.

Drink is at the heart of everything;
what made her love him
made her hate him in the end.

The Forever Relevance of Hope – Holly Bars

We met, two strangers, on my Grandma's couch, but you'll never know it. You were writing to me though, the template I am, pressed me between pages like they were fields, and I, a sentimental flower. We are so many, us Janes: lost girls, moor girls, who had our love chewed up and spat back out at us. Whose bones are still cold from all those fireless years. Much has changed. We have washing machines and mobile phones and takeaways, clean water and central heating. The loneliness though, it's not so different. I know, because you wrote it to me, and I found it. Author, I hear you. I'm living with an alcoholic parent, pillared and posted from one threshold to the next. Your book does not belong in my hands, on this well-sprung couch with cig-burned upholstery, smothered in cat hair, on a council estate, in Leeds; we were never meant to meet. And yet, Jane, she is mine, however much she insists she's no bird in no net. I hold her close to me; I feel her beating in my chest.

Raven – Tanya Nightingale

'How should I be if Providence had never given me courage enough to
adopt a career?… In that case I should have no world at all: the raven,
weary of surveying the deluge…would be my type. As it is, something
like a hope and motive sustains me still.' Charlotte Brontë, *Diary*

We circle the table
again and again
talking of Zamorna, and Rosina, and Jane.
We embroider, hem, and prove our bread
and plan out the lives we would have.
Our warm grey walls
absorb it all.

I circle the table
again and again
thinking of Arthur, and father, and Anne.
I patch their shirts and prove myself
and think of the life I now have.

The raven, in her black silk, follows.

A Visit to the Parsonage – Anne Caldwell

I find a plaited necklace of Anne's pale hair,
a matching bracelet with gold clasps,
holding the strands in place. Exhibit seven,
curled on velvet in an air-tight case,

Emily's darker hair's coiled in the same cabinet.
The blinds are drawn and rooms
are dusted, humidified, air
filtered to a constant temperature.
No draughts, no views of the moor's

bank of weather, gritstone and gullied peat.
There's a steady shuffle of die-hard Brontë fans,
taking phone-snaps, faces mooning in the glass.
What would Anne make of all of this?

I picture her as a child, striding
into the museum in sodden leather boots,
bonnet in hand, hair loose and wild,
yelling – *we sisters are not relics.*

I stare at the necklace and think of Scarborough,
TB blooming in Anne's lungs, riding a donkey
on the sands, with the most *glorious sunset*
ever witnessed from the lodging house.

Sewing with Charlotte – Hilary Robinson

I once saw her sewing box,
wooden, ordinary, lined with blue silk.
The usual stuff you'd expect to find —
reels of thread in muted shades,
buttons, lace, tape, paper packs
of needles and pins. No zips
of course — too early
for zips and press studs.
If I'd known Charlotte
I'd have sat happily beside her
sewing samplers, trying not to split
the words over line breaks.
If Charlotte were with me now
she'd help me thread
my new overlocker after
we'd watched YouTube clips.
She'd adore Vogue patterns.

Always Check the Top of the Wardrobe – Valerie Bence

I remember her wardrobe. I only looked in its dark depths once. The smell of mothballs was choking and her mother's astrakhan coat made me sneeze.

The top of it was deep in dust, probably not cleaned since the war; the old gas masks were still up there together with a box of clothes from the baby that died and his out of season hats. Nothing too exciting, so I never looked up there again

I did have a fascination with wardrobes though, there was one in their outhouse that I used to sit in, hiding when I should probably have been out, running wild like those moor-bound Brontë girls. Imagine looking on top of another wardrobe and finding this picture folded not rolled, deep creases bisect the sitters and there is little light relief. Anne especially, seems to be thinking of the many things she would rather be doing. A pillar like a green spotlight takes Branwell's place and I wonder – how unhappy do you have to be to erase yourself from your own painting?

Sixpenny Guide – Liz Mills

She came for the air,
the last that she'd breathe.
She followed her mother, her sister and brother
unaware of the legacy she'd leave.

She remained *where the flower fell,*
in sight of the castle and bay,
watched over by Coastguards' cottages
        – still visited even today.

Aged five, I swung on the gate,
greeting those who came to see what was left
of the little-known retiring sister,
who left Charlotte and Patrick bereft.

Her name meant little to me then
except for the words on the grave
in a place that was named Paradise
and the pennies I'd take home to save.

Contributor Biographies

Amina Alyal has published poetry widely, for example in *Iota*, *Dream Catcher*, *Aesthetica Review of Contemporary Artists*, *Metamorphic: 21st Century Poets Respond to Ovid*, and two collections, *The Ordinariness of Parrots* (Stairwell Books 2015) and *Season of Myths* (Wordspace at Indigo Dreams 2016). She has published scholarly research, most recently *Victorian Cultures of Liminality: Borders and Margins* (Cambridge Scholars 2019). She teaches creative writing and English at Leeds Trinity University. She is interested in working with the cross-overs, sometimes synaesthetic, between music, spoken and written word, and the visual image. She is currently working on two poetry collections, on ghosts and ecosystems.

Holly Bars is a mature student currently studying at the University of Leeds, where she is also co-editor for *Poetry & Audience*. Her poems have been published since January 2021 by *Ink, Sweat & Tears, Fragmented Voices, Porridge, Visual Verse, Anti-Heroin Chic, Runcible Spoon,* and more, as well as appearing in anthologies. She is currently working on her debut collection, *Dirty*.

Bob Beagrie (PhD) lives in Middlesbrough. He has published numerous collections of poetry and several pamphlets, most recently: *When We Wake We Think We're Whalers from Eden* (Stairwell Books 2021) *And Then We Saw The Daughter of the Minotaur* (The Black Light Engine Press 2020), *Civil Insolencies* (Smokestack 2019), *Remnants* written with Jane Burn (Knives, Forks & Spoons Press (2019), *This Game of Strangers* – written with Jane Burn (Wyrd Harvest Press 2017), *Leasungspell* (Smokestack 2016). His work has appeared in numerous anthologies and magazines and has been translated into Finnish, Urdu, Swedish, Dutch, Spanish, Estonian and Karelian.

Valerie Bence, after a university career, completed an MA in Poetry at MMU (2017). She is primarily an ekphrastic poet encompassing artworks, truth, memory, place and time. Her first collection was *Falling in love with a dead man* (Cinnamon Press 2019) and second *Overlap* (the Emma Press 2022). She has been shortlisted for the Poetry School/Nine Arches Primers 4 (2018), Fish Poetry (2019), longlisted for the Ginkgo Prize (2019) and has poems in several anthologies. She has worked with the British Museum and the Scott Polar Research Institute in Cambridge. She is a Mum and a Nonna and lives in Bucks.

Hannah-Freya Blake is a Leeds-based writer and academic with a PhD in Gothic Literature, for which she was awarded research excellence. Her research on horror and humour in the Gothic bleeds into her creative writing. She is fascinated by the blending of supposed opposites—of elegance and vulgarity, of melancholy and wit. Her short story, 'Old Jack', pays homage to Gothic aesthetics, and won the Creative Showcase at Sheffield's Reimagining the Gothic in 2018. Her debut novella, *Cake Craft*, will be published by Nyx Publishing in 2023, and will be accompanied by other queer Gothic short stories.

Penny Boxall's collections are *Ship of the Line* (which won the 2016 Edwin Morgan Poetry Award), *Who Goes There?* (Valley Press, 2018) and, with artist Naoko Matsubara, *In Praise of Hands* (2020, Ashmolean Museum). Poems from her work-in-progress have won the Mslexia Women's Poetry Competition and awards from the Authors' Foundation and New Writing North. She has held fellowships at Merton College (Oxford), Hawthornden Castle and Chateau de Lavigny (Switzerland), and is a Royal Literary Fund Fellow.

Carole Bromley lives in York. She has three collections with Smith/Doorstop and one with Valley Press. Poems in many magazines and anthologies. She has won the Bridport Prize, the Hamish Canham Award, the Brontë Society Literary Award, the Torbay Prize and the 2022 Caterpillar Prize for children's poetry. Carole has read and run workshops at festivals, including Aldeburgh, Bridlington, York, Ilkley as well as the Imagine Festival of Children's Literature in London. www.carolebromleypoetry.co.uk

Anne Caldwell is a freelance writer based in West Yorkshire with a passion for writing about place and ecological themes. She currently works for the Open University and as a Royal Literary Fund Fellow at the University of Huddersfield. Her latest collection of prose poems is *Alice and the North* Valley Press, 2020. She has also co-edited a book of essays on prose poetry with Oz Hardwick, called *Prose Poetry Theory and Practice* (Routledge 2022).

Mark Connors is an award-winning poet and novelist from Leeds, UK. Mark has had over 170 poems published in magazines, anthologies and webzines. His debut poetry pamphlet, *Life is a Long Song* was published by OWF Press in 2015. His first full length collection, *Nothing is Meant to be Broken*, was published by Stairwell Books in 2017. His second poetry collection, *Optics*, was published in 2019 by Yaffle. His novels, *Stickleback* and *Tom Tit and the Maniacs*, were published in 2016 and 2018. Mark is also a compere, a literary facilitator and a managing editor at Yaffle. His third collection, *Afters*, was published by Yaffle in 2021.

Rachel Davies is widely published in journals and anthologies and has been a prize-winner in several poetry competitions. Her debut pamphlet, *Every Day I Promise Myself*, was published by 4Word Press in December 2020. She is also one of three poets, along with Hilary Robinson and Tonia Bevins, in the first Dragon Spawn pamphlet *Some Mothers Do…* (Beautiful Dragons Press 2018). Rachel is co-ordinator of the Poetry Society Stanza for East Manchester and Tameside. She has an MA in Creative

Writing and a PhD in contemporary poetry, both from Manchester Metropolitan University.

Peter J Donnelly lives in York where he works as a hospital secretary. He has a degree in English Literature and a MA in Creative Writing from the University of Wales Lampeter. He has been published in various magazines and anthologies including *Dreich, Writer's Egg, Southlight, South Bank, Black Nore Review, One Hand Clapping* and the *High Window*. He came second in the 2021 Ripon Poetry Festival competition and was joint runner up in the Buzzwords Open Poetry 2020 competition

Maura Dooley's most recent book (with Elhum Shakerifar) is a translation into English of the poetry of the Iranian poet Azita Ghahreman, *Negative of a Group Photograph* (Bloodaxe.) *The Silvering* is her own most recent collection. A new book *Five Fifty-Five* (Bloodaxe) will be published in 2023. She teaches at Goldsmiths, University of London and she is a Fellow of the Royal Society of Literature.

Jane de Gay is Professor of English Literature at Leeds Trinity University and Co-Director (with Professor Karen Sayer) of the Leeds Centre for Victorian Studies. She is the author of *Virginia Woolf and Christian Culture* (Edinburgh University Press, 2018), and *Virginia Woolf's Novels and the Literary Past* (Edinburgh University Press), which examines Woolf's creative responses to a variety of precursors, including the Brontës. For many years, she has had the joy of teaching The Novels of the Brontës on the LCVS programme, MA in Victorian Studies.

Oz Hardwick is a European poet, photographer, occasional musician, and accidental academic, whose mum was born about four miles from Haworth. He was probably introduced to the Brontës through his granddad's love of poetry, though it might have been the Olivier/Oberon *Wuthering Heights* on TV sometime in early childhood. That one definitely left its mark. When push comes to shove, *Villette* is probably his favourite nineteenth-century novel, though he profoundly disagrees with Charlotte on the merits of Belgium. Oz is Professor of Creative Writing at Leeds Trinity University and remains at best a rudimentary bass guitarist. www.ozhardwick.co.uk

Helen Hill lives in Flintshire with her partner, Liz and two cats. She has been writing on and off since the age of 7 and has been published in several anthologies and magazines as well as on websites and local radio. Her work has been displayed in various exhibitions in Chester, Wales, her home town of Sheffield and most recently in the Poetry Pharmacy at Bishop's Castle. Helen has been a member of Chester Poets and the Cross Borders Stanza group for many years and was a member of the poetry performance group, Invisible Lipstick.

Donna Irving is a medical librarian and poet from Yorkshire. Her poems have featured in anthologies published by Bradford Poetry Foundation; Yaffle; Black Light Engine Room Press and Driech. Her debut pamphlet *Symmetry of Folklore* was published in 2021 by Yaffle Press. Her poems have been described as having surgical precision, both metaphorical and medicinal, with a beautiful lexicon and kitchen sink affection. This comes from her years of experience in designing systematic search strategies for healthcare staff, and in teaching critical reading to healthcare students. She also takes her notebooks on buses, cooks with abandon, and walks the moors.

Sheila Jacob has three children, five grandchildren, and lives in North Wales with her husband. She was born and raised in Birmingham and finds her working class Brummie childhood, adolescence and heritage a rich source of inspiration. She has been writing poetry on a regular basis since 2013. Her poems have been published in various UK magazines, Webzines and anthologies, most recently in *One Hand Clapping, The High Window* and *Spilling Cocoa Over Martin Amis*. Her poem 'St.

Anthony of Nechells' was Highly Commended in the Wolverhampton Literary Festival 2022.

Helen Kay, known on Facebook for her diva hen puppet, Nigella, in 2021-2, was shortlisted for the Canon Live Collection, highly commended in the Welsh Poetry Awards and one of five poets featured in the Brotherton anthology (Carcanet). She curates a project to support neuro-divergent poets: dyslexiapoetry.co.uk. Her pamphlet, *This Lexia & Other Languages (v. press)* was published in 2020. Twitter Helen KAy166.

Will Kemp has won several competitions, been well-placed in others and had four collections published as well as many poems in various journals including: *Ambit, The Guardian, Iota, Magma, The North* and *The Rialto.* He teaches Creative Writing at York University and judges the *Keats-Shelley Prize.* For details, visit: www.wkemp.com

Gill Lambert is a poet and teacher from Yorkshire. She has been widely published online and in print and her first collection *Tadaima* was published by Yaffle in 2019. Her second collection was recently published by Yaffle (*A Small Goodbye at Dawn,* 2022).

Jill Lang's love of words started as a teenager playing Scrabble with her father. Her paternal grandmother bought her books and shared her passion for letter-writing. At secondary school, two inspirational teachers taught Jill French and Spanish leading her to study Modern Languages at Leeds University. She first worked in publishing then, after three years' living in the USA and volunteering in a literacy programme, she trained as a French teacher. Since retiring, Jill has participated in creative writing courses and a weekly poetry workshop mainly writing for her own pleasure, grateful for the encouragement of tutors and peers.

Maggie Mackay's pamphlet *The Heart of the Run*, Picaroon Poetry, 2018 was followed by her full collection *A West Coast Psalter*, Kelsay Books, 2021. In 2020 she was awarded a place in the Poetry Archive's WordView permanent collection and, more recently, her poems have been highly commended in the Liverpool Poetry Prize Competition and longlisted in the Yaffle Press Prize. She reviews poetry pamphlets at https://sphinxreview.co.uk (Happenstance Press) and collections at The Friday Poem (https://thefridaypoem.com).
She can be found on Twitter @Bonniedreamer.

Liz Mills has been performing since she was 2 1/2 – poetry and Bible Reading when very young, then acting with amateur and semi-pro groups for many years – always happy to read other people's words. Teaching and acting left little time for writing! Then some years ago she started writing when she went to a Festival as a spectator, and hasn't looked back since. She has had some poetry published on line and in anthologies, but is still happiest performing, often on the same bill as her husband John, at venues from Lewes in the South to Callander in the North. She is looking for a publisher for her collection, *Clearance*.

Alison Milner lives on a steep, wooded hillside in Hebden Bridge, West Yorkshire. The sometimes desolate, but always stunningly beautiful, moorland between her home and Haworth is the canvas for much of her poetry and flash fiction. Alison enjoys having blank page time to play with words. She attends a WEA (Workers' Educational Association) creative writing group in the town, and the local 'writing buddy' community provides reciprocal encouragement and support. Her previous work has been published in *Lucent Dreaming* and *Briefly Write* literary magazines, as well as in the *When This Is All Over* and *One Minute Monologue* anthologies.

Jenny Mitchell is winner of the Poetry Book Awards 2021, and joint winner of the Geoff Stevens Memorial Prize 2019. Her poems have been widely published and have won numerous competitions, most recently the Inaugural Ironbridge Prize 2022. The best-selling debut collection, *Her Lost Language*, is One of 44 Poetry Books for 2019 (Poetry Wales). A second collection, *Map of a Plantation*, is an Irish Independent 'Literary Find'. Both books are on the syllabus of Manchester Metropolitan University. Her third collection is called *Resurrection of a Black Man*, published by Indigo Dreams.

Tanya Nightingale won the Yorkshire Open Poetry Competition in 2008. She is Reviews Editor for *Dream Catcher* and had poetry published in *Orbis, Acumen, Other Poetry and Poetry Nottingham*, amongst others. She appeared as guest writer on Helen Burke's radio show 'Word Salad' for East Leeds FM (twice) and has performed in International Women's Week with Real People Theatre. Tanya performed with Rose Drew in 'She's the Cultured One' at the Edinburgh Fringe in 2011, at the Galtres Festival in July 2013 and a specially-commissioned show at the Keats Shelley House in Rome in May 2014. Her first full-length poetry collection *The Problem with Beauty* appeared with Stairwell Books in September 2015. Despite a financial crisis and a pandemic, her next collection is well underway.

Wendy Pratt is a poet, author and workshop facilitator living and working in North Yorkshire. Her latest collection, *When I Think of My Body as a Horse*, won the Poetry Business Book and Pamphlet competition in 2021. Her non-fiction book, *The Ghost Lake,* was long listed in the Nan Shepherd prize 2021. She is the founder and editor in chief of *Spelt* Magazine, a print magazine dedicated to celebrating and validating the rural experience. She is represented by Portobello Books Literary Agency.

Jenny Robb has been writing poetry since retiring from a social work and management career, mainly in mental health services. Since 2020 she's been published widely in online and print magazines and in anthologies. Her debut collection, The Doll's Hospital, Yaffle Press 2022, has recently been published. She lives in Liverpool with her partner and the family cat and has one grown-up daughter. Twitter: @jirobb

Hilary Robinson's publications include *The Interpreter's House, Obsessed with Pipework, Strix, Morning Star, Atrium* and *Poetry Birmingham* and several anthologies including *Please Hear What I'm Not Saying* (Fly on the Wall Poetry 2018), *A New Manchester Alphabet* (Manchester Writing School 2015) and *Bloody Amazing!* (Yaffle/Beautiful Dragons Press 2020). In 2018 her poems were published in the first DragonSpawn book, *Some Mothers Do . . .* with Rachel Davies and Tonia Bevins. Hilary collaborates with composers and, during lockdown, wrote an opera libretto. In June 2021, Hilary's pamphlet, *Revelation*, was published by 4Word Press. Hilary has an MA in Creative Writing from MMU.

Su Ryder is a poet and writer of short fiction, from Leeds, West Yorkshire. Her poem 'Behind the Pond, Meanwoodside' won first prize in the 2021 Leeds Poetry Festival Competition and appeared in the festival's anthology *At Home in Our City*. Su's poetry has also been published in the Saboteur Award winning *Bloody Amazing* (Dragon Yaffle), the 2020 Leeds Literature Festival anthology *And the Stones Fell Open* (Yaffle), also in *Strix*, and *Visual Verse*. Her short fiction has also been published in the *Dark Lane Anthologies* and *Neon Magazine*.

Edwin Stockdale has an MA in Creative Writing with Distinction from the University of Birmingham. Widely published in the UK, his work includes two pamphlets with Red Squirrel Press: *Aventurine* (2014) and *The Glower of the Sun* (2019). Scholarly articles drawn from his practice-based research have appeared in *Writing in Practice* and a book chapter in *Prose Poetry in Theory and Practice* (Routledge, May 2022). Recently, he was the first person to gain PhD in Creative Writing (Poetry) at Leeds Trinity University and was awarded a major grant from Arts Council England through the Developing Your Creative Practice fund to complete a collection of poetry about Edward II.

Hannah Stone, an alumna of the first MA Creative Writing programme at Leeds Trinity University, has published four solo volumes of poetry, plus a number of co-authored collaborations (for Stairwell, Indigo Dreams Publishing, Maytree Press and Runcible Spoon) and is also represented in numerous anthologies and journals, both in the UK and internationally. She collaborates with composer Matthew Oglesby; convenes poetry events including for the Leeds Library and Leeds Lieder Festival; and is poet-theologian in residence for the Leeds Church Institute. She edits Dream Catcher literary journal. She may be contacted for book sales, workshops, and readings on hannahstone14@hotmailcom

Kathleen Strafford is a graduate of Trinity University holding an MA in Creative Writing. She has been widely published on webzines and anthologies. Her first collection of poetry *Her Own Language* was published by Dempsey and Windle in 2017. Kathleen's second collection *Wilderness of Skin* was published by Yaffle in 2019.She is the chief editor of Runcible Spoon Webzine and publishing. Her new collection *Girl in the Woods* and pamphlet *Life Under Glass* will be published this year.

Angela Topping is the author of eight collections and four pamphlets of poetry. A former Writer in Residence at Gladstone's Library, she also writes critical books on literary texts, for Greenwich Exchange. She was educated at Liverpool University, where she also completed a post-graduate degree in Victorian Studies. She has edited a pamphlet of poems on the

Brontës published by Like This Press, entitled *The Scratching of Pens* (2014) alongside ones on Austen and Shakespeare. Her work has appeared in numerous journals and anthologies, featured on Poetry Please, and been set for A level. A former English teacher, she now works freelance.

Clint Wastling's poetry has been widely published in magazines and anthologies. Maytree Press published his first poetry collection *Layers*. He is currently working as poet in residence at Burton Constable Hall. Clint has a full collection of poetry called *Quiet Flows the Hull,* coming out in late 2022. His novel, *The Geology of Desire,* is an LGBTQ thriller set around Whitby in the 1980's and Hull during World War II. He also has a sci-fi novel, *Tyrants Rex,* set 3000 years in the future. Both are published by Stairwell Books.

Clare Wigzell is a Leeds-based poet who writes poetry in response to place, nature and works of art. She is currently writing and performing poetry about Kirkstall Abbey and Turner. She is also writing in response to Hepworth's sculpture. She has been published in a number of anthologies with Indigo Dreams, Leeds Trinity University and Wordspace. She collaborates separately with a book artist, a composer and a photographer.

Eva Wigzell has been writing short stories and poetry for around seven years. Currently thirteen, she is particularly interested in building characters in both her stories and poetry. Before this poem was written, she went Scarborough with her grandmother, who is also included in this anthology, on an Anne Brontë tour. During this, she found that the combination of experiencing the sea and learning about Anne Brontë inspired her. Other than writing, Eva is passionate about art and hopes to illustrate her work in the future. This is her first publication and she wishes to continue writing in many forms.

Sarah Wimbush's poetry is rooted in Yorkshire with tales of childhood, colliery villages and Gypsies and Travellers. She has published two prize-winning pamphlets: *Bloodlines* (Seren, 2020) and *The Last Dinosaur in Doncaster* (Smith | Doorstop, 2021). She won the 2021 Poetry Society Stanza Competition and her poems have appeared in *Brittle Star, The Interpreter's House, The North, Stand* and *Wagtail: The Roma Women's Poetry Anthology* (Butcher's Dog, 2021). *Shelling Peas with My Grandmother in the Gorgiolands* is her first book-length collection (Bloodaxe, 2022).

Gregory Woods is the author of *We Have the Melon* (1992), *May I Say Nothing* (1998), *The District Commissioner's Dreams* (2002), *Quidnunc* (2007), *An Ordinary Dog* (2011), and *Records of an Incitement to Silence* (2021), all from Carcanet Press. His cultural histories include *Articulate Flesh: Male Homoeroticism and Modern Poetry* (1987), *A History of Gay Literature: The Male Tradition* (1998) and *Homintern: How Gay Culture Liberated the Modern World* (2016), all from Yale University Press. In 1998 he became the first Professor of Gay & Lesbian Studies in the UK, at Nottingham Trent University, where he is still Professor Emeritus.

Lucy Wright is a PhD candidate in Creative Writing at Leeds Trinity University. She writes prose and poetry in a selection of genres from experimental surrealism, magical realism and historical fiction. During her MA, she has been accepted for three publications. Most recently being a charity magazine *Queer, There and Everywhere* for LGBTQ creatives with the others due to be published in the upcoming months. Though she can often be found in bookshops, galleries and museums across Yorkshire, Lucy extends those interests back home in the northeast with her family.

Indigo Dreams Publishing Ltd
24, Forest Houses
Cookworthy Moor
Halwill
Beaworthy
Devon
EX21 5UU
www.indigodreamspublishing.com